Post your finished work and join the community.

#FAITHINCOLOR

SCENES FROM THE PSALMS

ADULT COLORING BOOK

COLOR the Comfort of God's Care and Protection

PASSIO

The most valuable thing the Psalms do for me is to express

the same delight in God which made David dance.

—C. S. LEWIS

Let Your Heart Sing Praises...

The one hundred fifty psalms included in the Bible's Book of Psalms are attributed to several authors, but the most famous by far is David. The shepherd turned king is known for how he opened his heart to God. Even on days when he felt alone and struggled, David called out to God and found reasons to praise Him.

Throughout history, many people have taken comfort in the psalms. Originally written as songs, their lyrical, poetic style has made them a longstanding favorite for quoting and memorizing. Many of the psalms focus on praise and thanksgiving to God for all that He has done and all that He promises to do. It is these psalms in particular that have been gathered and included in this special coloring book.

Our intention is that as you color, you will think back to times in your past when knowing that God is in complete control brought you through a seemingly hopeless situation or tough problem. Perhaps you didn't see it at the time, but in looking back, you are now able to thank Him for His faithfulness. Record these memories in this book or a journal. Praising God for His faithfulness will build your faith, helping you believe that He is able to meet every need that you face now or in your future. You can trust Him and continue to praise Him. And when you do, His peace, "which surpasses all understanding, will protect your hearts and minds through Christ Jesus" (Phil. 4:7).

We've placed these carefully selected verses from the Book of Psalms on the facing page of each design. Each one was chosen to complement the illustration while inspiring you to lift your own praises to God with a grateful heart. As you color these designs, reflect quietly on God's goodness and the many gifts He has bestowed upon you. When you are encouraged by God's promises to love and care for you, you will find that the cares and worries of life melt away.

It might interest you to know that the verses in this book are taken from the Modern English Version of the Holy Bible. The Modern English Version (MEV) is the most modern translation produced in the King James tradition within the last thirty years. This formal equivalence translation maintains the beauty of the past yet provides fresh clarity for a new generation of Bible readers. If you would like more information on the MEV, please visit www.mevbible.com.

We hope you find this coloring book to be both beautiful and inspirational. As you color, remember that the best artistic endeavors have no rules. Unleash your creativity as you experiment with colors, textures, and mediums. Freedom of self-expression will help to release wellness, balance, mindfulness, and inner peace into your life, allowing you to enjoy the process as well as the finished product. When you're finished, you can frame your favorite creations for displaying or gift giving. Then post your artwork on Facebook, Twitter, or Instagram with the hashtag #FAITHINCOLOR.

Blessed is the man who walks not in the counsel of the ungodly…his delight is in the law of the Lord.

—PSALM 1:1–2, MEV

*You, O L*ORD*, are a shield for me, my glory and the One who*

*raises up my head. I cried to the L*ORD *with my voice, and*

He answered me from His holy hill.

*—P*SALM *3:3–4,* MEV

You, O Lord, are a Shield for Me

PSALM 3:3–4

O Lord, in the morning You will hear my voice; in the morning I will direct my prayer to You, and I will watch expectantly.

—Psalm 5:3, MEV

When I consider Your heavens, the work of Your

fingers, the moon and the stars, which You have

established, what is man that You are mindful of him,

and the son of man that You attend to him?

—P*SALM 8:3–4,* MEV

I will give thanks to You, O LORD, with my whole heart; I will declare all Your marvelous works.

—PSALM 9:1, MEV

I love You, O LORD, my strength. The LORD is my pillar, and my fortress, and my deliverer; my God, my rock, in whom I take refuge; my shield, and the horn of my salvation, my high tower.

—*PSALM 18:1–2, MEV*

You have lengthened my stride under me,

so that my feet did not slip.

—PSALM 18:36, MEV

The heavens declare the glory of God,

and the firmament shows His handiwork.

—PSALM 19:1, MEV

The Glory of God

GOD

Psalm 19:1

Some trust in chariots, and some in horses,

but we will remember the name of the LORD our God.

—PSALM 20:7, MEV

The LORD is my shepherd; I shall not want. He makes

me lie down in green pastures; He leads me beside still

waters. He restores my soul.

—PSALM 23:1–3, MEV

The earth belongs to the Lord, and its fullness, the world, and those who dwell in it. For He has founded it on the seas, and established it on the floods.

—Psalm 24:1–2, MEV

The LORD is my light and my salvation; whom will I fear?

The LORD is the strength of my life; of whom will I be afraid?

—PSALM 27:1, MEV

The
LORD
is my *light*
and my
salvation...

❧ PSALM 27:1 ❧

Your mercy, O LORD, is in the heavens,

and Your faithfulness reaches to the clouds.

—PSALM 36:5, MEV

For with You is the fountain of life;

in Your light we see light.

—P*salm* 36:9, *mev*

For with You is the fountain of life;

in Your light we see light.

PSALM 36:9

As the deer pants after the water brooks,

so my soul pants after You, O God.

—PSALM 42:1, MEV

O my God, my soul is cast down within me; therefore I will remember You from the land of Jordan, and of the Hermon, from the hill of Mizar. Deep calls to deep at the noise of Your waterfalls; all Your waves and Your billows passed over me.

—PSALM 42:6–7, MEV

Be still and know that I am God.

—PSALM *46:10,* MEV

In God I trust, I will not fear; what can a man do to me?

—Psalm 56:11, MEV

For Your mercy is great up to the heavens, and Your truth extends to the clouds. Be exalted, O God, above the heavens; may Your glory be above all the earth.

—PSALM 57:10–11, MEV

I will sing of Your power; I will sing aloud of Your

lovingkindness in the morning, for You have been

my refuge and escape in the day of my trouble.

—P*SALM* 59:16, *MEV*

Trust in Him at all times; you people, pour out your heart before Him; God is a shelter for us.

—Psalm 62:8, MEV

Because You have been my help, therefore in the

shadow of Your wings I will rejoice.

*—P*SALM *63:7,* MEV

You, who are the confidence of all the ends of the earth, and of those who are afar off on the sea; who established the mountains by His strength, being clothed with might; who stills the noise of the seas.

—PSALM 65:5–7, MEV

You visit the earth, and water it; You enrich it

with the river of God, which is full of water.

—PSALM 65:9, MEV

Shout joyfully to God, all you lands! Sing out the glory

of His name; make His praise glorious.

—Psalm 66:1–2, MEV

Sing out the Glory of His name...

PSALM 66:2

Whom have I in heaven but You? And there is nothing on earth that I desire besides You. My flesh and my heart fails, but God is the strength of my heart and my portion forever.

—Psalm 73:25–26, MEV

The day is Yours, the night also is Yours; You have prepared the light and the sun. You have established all the borders of the earth; You have made summer and winter.

—PSALM 74:16–17, MEV

For the LORD *God is a sun and shield; the* LORD *will give favor and glory, for no good thing will He withhold from the one who walks uprightly.*

*—*PSALM *84:11,* MEV

Design your own crest inside the shield on the next page,
and write your name on the banner below.

The heavens are Yours; the earth also is Yours;

the world and all that is in it, You have founded them.

—PSALM 89:11, MEV

For a thousand years in Your sight are but as yesterday

when it is past, or as a night watch in the night time.

—PSALM 90:4, MEV

*I will say of the L*ORD,

"He is my refuge and my fortress, my God in whom I trust."

—*P*SALM *91:2,* MEV

He shall cover you with His feathers, and

under His wings you shall find protection; His

faithfulness shall be your shield and wall.

—PSALM 91:4, MEV

He shall cover you with His feathers,

AND UNDER His wings YOU SHALL FIND Protection

PSALM 91:4

When I said, "My foot slips,"

Your mercy, O Lord, held me up.

—*Psalm 94:18,* mev

In His hand are the deep places of the earth; the heights of the mountains are also His. The sea is His, for He made it, and His hands formed the dry land.

—PSALM 95:4–5, MEV

Let the heavens rejoice, and let the earth be glad; let the sea roar, and all that fills it; let the field be joyful, and all that is in it; then all the trees of the forests shall rejoice before the LORD.

—PSALM 96:11–13, MEV

Know that the LORD, He is God; it is He who

has made us, and not we ourselves; we are His

people, and the sheep of His pasture.

—PSALM 100:3, MEV

You send the springs to gush forth in the valleys,

which flow between the hills.

—Psalm 104:10, MEV

You cause the grass to grow for the cattle and plants for the cultivation of man....The trees of the Lord are well watered, the cedars of Lebanon that He has planted.

—*Psalm 104:14–16,* MEV

O Lord, how manifold are Your works! With wisdom You have made them all; the earth is full of Your creatures— so is this great and wide sea, which is full of innumerable creatures, living animals both small and great.

—Psalm 104:24–25, mev

From the rising of the sun to its going down,

the Lord's name is to be praised.

—Psalm 113:3, MEV

I love the LORD, because He has heard my voice and my

supplications. Because He has inclined His ear to me,

therefore I will call upon Him as long as I live.

—PSALM *116:1–2,* MEV

This is the day that the L<small>ORD</small> has made;

we will rejoice and be glad in it.

—P<small>SALM</small> 118:24, <small>MEV</small>

The Lord is God, and He has shown us His light.

—Psalm 118:27, MEV

Whatever the Lord pleases, He does in heaven and on earth,

in the seas and all the depths. He causes the clouds to ascend

from the ends of the earth; He makes lightning for the rain.

—Psalm 135:6–7, MEV

The Lord is good to all,

and His compassion is over all His works.

—Psalm 145:9, MEV

The LORD is good to all, and His compassion is over all His works.

PSALM 145:9

He heals the broken in heart, and binds up their

wounds. He counts the number of the stars;

He calls them all by their names.

—Psalm 147:3–4, MEV

He counts the number of the stars; He calls them all by their names.

PSALM 147:4

Most Charisma House Book Group products are available at special quantity discounts for bulk purchase for sales promotions, premiums, fund-raising, and educational needs. For details, write Charisma House Book Group, 600 Rinehart Road, Lake Mary, Florida 32746, or telephone (407) 333-0600.

Scenes From the Psalms published by Passio
Charisma Media/Charisma House Book Group
600 Rinehart Road
Lake Mary, Florida 32746
www.charismahouse.com

All Scripture quotations are taken from the Holy Bible, Modern English Version. Copyright © 2014 by Military Bible Association. Used by permission. All rights reserved.

Design Director: Justin Evans
Cover Design: Justin Evans
Interior Design: Justin Evans, Lisa Rae McClure, Vincent Pirozzi

Illustrations: Getty Images/Depositphotos

C. S. Lewis quote taken from *Reflections on the Psalms* (London, England: Fount, 1998), 39.

International Standard Book Number: 978-1-62998-778-1

This publication is translated in Spanish under the title *Escenas de los Salmos*, copyright © 2016, published by Casa Creación, a Charisma Media company. All rights reserved.

First edition

16 17 18 19 20 — 987654321

Printed in the United States of America